This Hieroglyphic Journal Belongs to:

_____

How to use this journal

In this hieroglyphic journal, you will find left-hand pages with graph lines and standard, lined right-hand pages. This layout was especially designed for people like you, who are learning how to read and write Egyptian hieroglyphs.

To get the most out of the format of this journal, use the left-hand pages to draw the hieroglyphs of the text you are studying or the exercise (such as from a textbook) you are working through. The graph-paper-like layout will help you to form your hieroglyphs.

On the right-hand page, write your transliteration and translation of the hieroglyphic text you wrote on the left side.

Each set of pages also includes a place to note the date, the text you are working on, and which lines of the text (or which exercise) you completed on that page.

Use these info boxes at the tops of pages and the index at the front of the journal to record what you worked on where. This will allow you to return to your journal later and easily find what you're looking for at a glance.

Example

Date: 1/1/20
Text: Shipwrecked Sailor
Lines: 1 - 4

Example

2

<u>ḏd.in šmsw iḳr wḏз ib=k ḥзti-ꜥ</u>
Then the excellent follower said:
" Be of good cheer, governor!"

The quote used on the cover and bottoms of pages in this hieroglyphs practice journal comes from the first maxim of the Maxims of Ptahhotep.

It translates to: "Good speech is more rare than green stone, (yet) may be found (even) with the servants at the grindstone."*

In other words, eloquence is rare, but anyone can become eloquent, regardless of background - an appropriate sentiment for those of us learning a foreign language and writing system.

The scribal palette hieroglyph in the center of the cover spells the words for "writing" and "scribe."

To start learning hieroglyphs, download my free guide: http://bit.ly/hieroglyphsguide

*dg3 md(w)t nfrt r w3d iw gm.t(w).s mꜥ ḥmwt ḥr bnwt

Index

Text   Page

Index

Text	Page

Index

Text	Page

Index

Text	Page

Index

Text	Page

1

13

Date: _____

Text: _____

Lines: _____

23

Date: _____

Text: _____

Lines: _____

Date: _____

Text: _____

Lines: _____

Date: _____

Text: _____

Lines: _____

Date: _____

Text: _____

Lines: _____

Date: _____

Text: _____

Lines: _____

Date:

Text:

Lines:

Date: _____

Text: _____

Lines: _____

39

Date: _____

Text: _____

Lines: _____

Date: _____

Text: _____

Lines: _____

49

Date: _____

Text: _____

Lines: _____

Date: _____

Text: _____

Lines: _____

Date: _____

Text: _____

Lines: _____

Date: _____

Text: _____

Lines: _____

59

Date: _____

Text: _____

Lines: _____

Date: _____

Text: _____

Lines: _____

65

Date: _____

Text: _____

Lines: _____

Date: _____

Text: _____

Lines: _____

Date: _____

Text: _____

Lines: _____

Date: _____

Text: _____

Lines: _____

Date: _____

Text: _____

Lines: _____

75

Date: _____

Text: _____

Lines: _____

Date: _____

Text: _____

Lines: _____

79

Date: _____

Text: _____

Lines: _____

81

Date: _____

Text: _____

Lines: _____

Date: _____

Text: _____

Lines: _____

Date: _____

Text: _____

Lines: _____

Date: _____

Text: _____

Lines: _____

Date: _____

Text: _____

Lines: _____

91

Date: _____

Text: _____

Lines: _____

Date: _____

Text: _____

Lines: _____

97

Date: _____
Text: _____
Lines: _____

Date: _____

Text: _____

Lines: _____

Date: _____

Text: _____

Lines: _____

103

Date:

Text:

Lines:

107

Date:

Text:

Lines:

Date: _____

Text: _____

Lines: _____

Date: _____

Text: _____

Lines: _____

Date: _____

Text: _____

Lines: _____

Date:

Text:

Lines:

Date: _____

Text: _____

Lines: _____

Date: _____

Text: _____

Lines: _____

Date: _____

Text: _____

Lines: _____

Date:

Text:

Lines:

133

Date:

Text:

Lines:

Date: _____

Text: _____

Lines: _____

137

Date:

Text:

Lines:

Date: _____

Text: _____

Lines: _____

Date: _____

Text: _____

Lines: _____

Date: _____

Text: _____

Lines: _____

Date: _____

Text: _____

Lines: _____

Date: _____

Text: _____

Lines: _____

Date:

Text:

Lines:

Date: _____

Text: _____

Lines: _____

Date: _____

Text: _____

Lines: _____

155

Date: _____

Text: _____

Lines: _____

Date: _____

Text: _____

Lines: _____

_____
_____
_____
_____
_____
_____
_____
_____
_____
_____
_____
_____
_____
_____
_____
_____
_____
_____
_____
_____

Date: _____

Text: _____

Lines: _____

Date: _____

Text: _____

Lines: _____

Date: _____

Text: _____

Lines: _____

Date:

Text:

Lines:

167

Date:

Text:

Lines:

Date: _____

Text: _____

Lines: _____

Date: _____

Text: _____

Lines: _____

Date: _____

Text: _____

Lines: _____

177

Date: _____

Text: _____

Lines: _____

181

Date: _____

Text: _____

Lines: _____

Date: _____

Text: _____

Lines: _____

Date: _____

Text: _____

Lines: _____

Date: _____

Text: _____

Lines: _____

189

191

Date:

Text:

Lines:

Date: _____

Text: _____

Lines: _____

Date: _____

Text: _____

Lines: _____

Date: _____

Text: _____

Lines: _____

Date: _____

Text: _____

Lines: _____

The quote used on the cover and bottoms of pages in this hieroglyphs practice journal comes from the first maxim of the Maxims of Ptahhotep.

It translates to: "Good speech is more rare than green stone, (yet) may be found (even) with the servants at the grindstone."*

In other words, eloquence is rare, but anyone can become eloquent, regardless of background - an appropriate sentiment for those of us learning a foreign language and writing system.

The scribal palette hieroglyph in the center of the cover spells the words for "writing" and "scribe."

To start learning hieroglyphs, download my free guide: http://bit.ly/hieroglyphsguide

*dg3 md(w)t nfrt r w3ḏ iw gm.t(w).s mꜥ ḥmwt ḥr bnwt